Nuffield Maths

EARLY CHALLENGERS

Susan E. Sanders

Contents

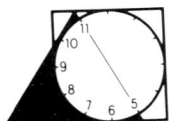

Nuffield Maths

General editor: Eric A Albany

LONGMAN

Introduction

This book is written for teachers of children in the first years of schooling. It is based on the belief that even very young children can be 'mathematicians' rather than mere calculators and introduces activities that emphasise the
'do, examine, predict, test, generalise' sequence
rather than the **'learn, practise, consolidate'** sequence.
The activities contain opportunities to develop and use skills of calculation and measuring, but these are a by-product rather than the main aim.

Many of the activities are appropriate for various ages and it is how they are introduced to the pupils and the context in which the *Starter* is set that will tailor them for a specific class. This is left to the individual teacher who will consider the intended aims and objectives for the activity before deciding on the framework in which it will be set.

Some suggestions are made for the appropriate organisations of the activities. These are not necessarily the only ways in which to introduce the work but are suggested for those teachers who, before experimenting with their own ideas, would like to follow a format that others have found useful.

The development of each *Starter* is also offered as a suggestion. Often this type of work develops as the lesson progresses but some will find it reassuring to have a possible structure before embarking on an untried idea. If other strands develop, it is up to the individual teacher to decide whether or not to take them up at that point. If suggestions have been made that would lead quickly to more advanced and complex mathematical ideas, this is indicated in the text.

Also included are photocopiable worksheets to accompany the *Starter* where this would be useful. Worksheets do not accompany those activities which are intended to develop pupils' own recording skills: they are included where the drawing of outlines could be very time consuming for either teacher or pupil.

The *Starters* are not in any particular developmental order but by cross-referencing to the National Curriculum and to the Nuffield Maths 5–11 Project it is hoped that the selection by the teacher of an appropriate *Starter* will be simplified. Where *Starters* are connected by a number pattern, a theme or topic, this is indicated in the text.

All the ideas have been tried out with pupils between the ages of 5 and 8 years. As indicated in the text, some of them have been tried with pupils below and above this age. They have been tried with the complete mainstream ability range and it has been reported frequently that performance with these sorts of activities can be very different to performance in more formal mathematical work.

Some of the activities are structured for an intended outcome. This is to allow specific mathematical skills to be developed. However, there may be other possible outcomes from a *Starter*; so care should be taken when responding to pupils' suggestions that do not lead towards the intended outcome. The compiling of a 'Class Book of Ideas' that may be used at a later date or by individual pupils in a free choice time, can be profitable. In this way, the ideas of individual pupils are given value and a resource for future work is built up. Also this allows time for teachers to explore suggestions 'in private' if they feel uncomfortable about following ideas that lead into an unfamiliar area. Other activities are more open-ended in nature and it is hoped that teachers will try both types of *Starters* as their experience with this sort of work develops.

Several general mathematical ideas are introduced to the pupils. These are indicated by use of **BOLD CAPITALS** in the text. The spotting of pattern has perhaps become very familiar in recent years but this is by no means the only, or even the first, question that should be considered. In fact, it can be very misleading to look for a pattern with only a small number of examples.

In this book, examples have been chosen so that a pattern can be spotted at the point suggested, but it is important that teachers stress the need to collect a good number of examples before looking for a pattern.

It is also important that pupils do more than just look for patterns. For this reason there are activities which allow pupils to ask '**WHAT IF?**', to **PREDICT**, to **TEST A HYPOTHESIS** and to **GENERALISE**.

WHAT IF? is used to indicate that pupils could consider other possible avenues of enquiry in a creative way. It is shorthand for the question 'What would happen if . . .?', suggested in Attainment Targets 1 and 9 of the National Curriculum.

PREDICT invites pupils to suggest what they think might happen next – often this will be asking for the next number in a series. When this prediction is checked, the pupils may be thought to be **TESTING A HYPOTHESIS**. Sometimes an activity will require that pupils devise a **FAIR TEST**. Both of these notions are included in the National Curriculum for Science as part of the Attainment Target 1.

After spotting a pattern in a series of numbers, it is appropriate in some activities to encourage pupils to **GENERALISE**: that is to look for the general relationship between the starting point and the outcome. For example, in *Starter 4*, using two dice, there are three ways to score 4, four ways to score 5, five ways to score 6, and so on. In this case the generalisation is that the number of ways to score a number is always one less than the score. In symbolic form, this would be written as $W = S - 1$, where W is the number of ways and S is the score we are trying to make. But we would not expect this expression from young children! Neither is the idea of formal proof considered appropriate.

Sometimes teachers will wish to use much simpler questions in order to develop mathematical language or check understanding. Activities are included that lend themselves to this approach. Other *Starters* would be diminished and much of the value lost if only simple questions are asked. It is important to remember that there tends to be an over-emphasis on the use of closed questions requiring only one word answers in our teaching and that pupils will often manipulate the teacher to reword more complex questions until they only require simple answers. Many of the *Starters* are offered as opportunities for pupils to develop higher order questioning and answering skills. They have proved successful where teachers have been careful to maintain their aims.

Some of the *Starters* can be introduced during an informal session 'on the mat' and where the activity runs over an extended time period – such as a morning, day or week – the use of a similar session at the end can be an excellent way to draw the strands together and for pupils to develop their communication and descriptive skills.

Some of these ideas have been used as the basis of assemblies and attractive displays, particularly where they have been set in the context of a theme or topic; for example, *Starter 8: Polyominoes*, *Starter 9: Multilink* and *Starter 14: Noah's Ark* were used in a topic on animals where the polyominoes became fields. The Multilink shapes became animals from other planets – those made from four pieces were from Planet Tetra, those made from five pieces from Planet Penta, and so on. Such media have been used as informal INSET vehicles and all the ideas in the book have been used in a variety of forms of professional development or shared with parents as a way of demonstrating the value of such work.

This book is produced in the hope that it will encourage teachers to have a go at work of a general mathematical nature with young children. The rewards to both teacher and pupils can be high. Teachers have expressed the need for a source of ideas that gives them a supportive structure as they develop this way of working. It is in response to such requests that this book is offered and your reactions to it are awaited eagerly.

Susan E. Sanders

STARTER 1: Towers

You need:

10 Unifix cubes of colour A and 10 Unifix cubes of colour B for each child (in groups of 4);
copies of Sheets 1A, 1B and 1C 'Towers' on pages 35–37.

Organisation

This activity can be done individually but it lends itself particularly to working in pairs and groups. A group of four works well. The activity can be used to develop the skill of working as a member of a group. The following is a suggested structure for achieving this.

Sit four children around a table. Each child has a partner. The 80 Unifix cubes (40 of colour A and 40 of colour B) should be easily accessible in the centre of the table.

The basic idea

Ask each child to build a tower that is three cubes high. (Unifix cubes are suggested so that it is obvious what is meant by a tower. See picture.)

Tell them to show that tower to their partner.
They must both be different, i.e. use different colour combinations (e.g. aaa or bbb or aba etc.). If they are not, one must change.

If you wish the pupils to work in pairs, now ask them to build as many different towers as they can that are three cubes high.

If you wish to develop co-operative work between more pupils, ask the group to look at each other's towers. Any that are the same must now be changed. The group now works on the task of building all possible towers.
When a group appears to be satisfied that they have completed the task, they can be asked to record the results on worksheet 1A.

Most groups will finish around the same time: particularly if you have supported as appropriate during the activity.

Ask each group in turn how many towers they have built and all should have succeeded in building 8. The fact that with two colours and towers three cubes high you can build 8 towers should now be recorded. Teacher recording on the board is appropriate.

You can now ask the '**WHAT IF?**' question.

Children will suggest several changes. These may include: change the number of cubes in the tower or change the number of colours. Another suggestion may be to change the Unifix for Multilink. This idea is explored in *Starter 9*.

It is probably easiest to explore the idea of changing the number of cubes in the tower.

This generates a manageable number of towers and a simple pattern of increase.

At this point you could either ask each group to **INVESTIGATE** what happens if they build towers of different heights or you could give different groups different height towers to build.

The first option gives opportunities for more open-ended activity and the second option allows you to present tasks appropriate to the ability of a group.

Developments

As groups build complete sets of towers, you can record this on the board. Do not forget the smaller number option.

The pattern that emerges (for towers using two colours) is:

1 cube high   2 towers
2 cubes high   4 towers
3 cubes high   8 towers
4 cubes high   16 towers.

The pupils may now be at a point where they can **PREDICT** the next answer. (The number of towers is doubling.)

A larger group can now **TEST** the prediction. This could be over an extended time scale.

5 cubes high   32 towers.

If you are working with particularly bright pupils at the top of the age range you may find that they can **GENERALISE**. Remind them that they are looking for a connection between the number of colours (2), the number of cubes and the number of towers.

Remember you are looking for an explanation not an algebraic expression! Explanations will tend to be . . . 'You multiply the number of colours by itself the same number of times as the number of cubes in the tower.'

i.e. $2 \times 2 = 4$
          $2 \times 2 \times 2 = 8$
         $2 \times 2 \times 2 \times 2 = 16$

Formally, $T = 2^N$ where T is the number of towers and N is the number of colours. But we do not expect this from the pupils!

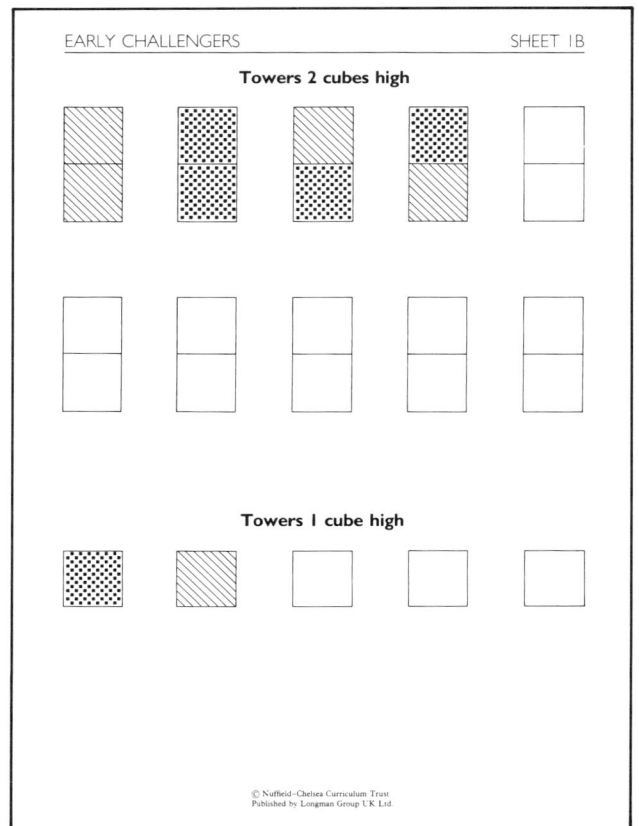

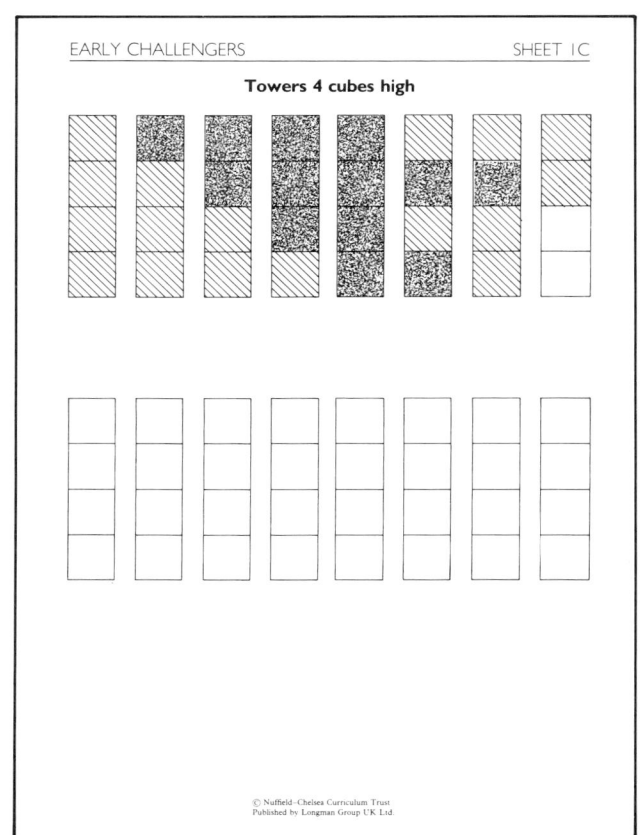

Changing the number of colours and keeping towers three cubes high results in the pattern:

1 colour	1 tower	$1 \times 1 \times 1 = 1$
2 colours	8 towers	$2 \times 2 \times 2 = 8$
3 colours	27 towers	$3 \times 3 \times 3 = 27$
4 colours	64 towers	$4 \times 4 \times 4 = 64$

The number of towers is the number of colours multiplied by itself three times.

Formally, $T = N^3$.

This generates a large number of towers very quickly and that is why the first alternative is suggested as an initial activity.

National Curriculum Targets

Attainment Target 1: Levels 1, 2, 3
Attainment Target 2: Level 1
Attainment Target 3: Level 3
Attainment Target 4: Level 3

Nuffield Scheme Cross-reference

Nuffield Maths 2 Teachers' Handbook   N11

STARTER 2: Dolls

You need:

Three dolls dressed in different colours in up to four items of clothing; copies of Sheet 2 on page 38. (Choose the most appropriate version for your style of dolls, e.g. Western; Sikh; Muslim.)

Organisation

This is an activity that lends itself to an informal introduction from the teacher to any size group of children. With younger children you should aim to allow them to dress dolls, but with older pupils you could demonstrate the idea and allow them to use the more abstract experience of using paper dolls and clothes or colouring in outline drawings, as suggested, for recording findings.

The basic idea

Show each doll in an outfit consisting of the same two items; skirt and jumper or shalwar and trousers.

Suggest the idea that the dolls can swap clothes. Let a child change the way the dolls are dressed. Ask other children to repeat until there are no more suggestions. Then ask how many different ways the dolls have been dressed.

Each doll can be dressed in four different ways.

This can be recorded using Sheet 2, or by using Unifix cubes to represent the items and colour of clothing, or by displaying the dolls if you have enough.

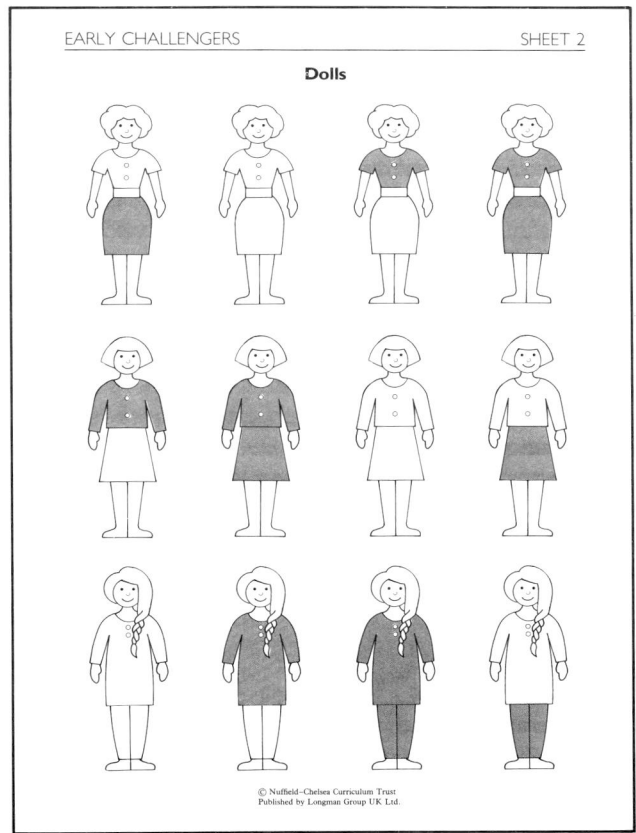

This can now be developed in a variety of ways:
- you could investigate what happens if you change the number of dolls;
- you could investigate what happens if you change the number of items of clothing.

The children may well suggest both of these when you ask the '**WHAT IF?**' question.

It is important to be very careful about the exact question you ask next if you have a specific outcome in mind. 'How many ways can you dress the dolls?' and 'How many ways can you dress each doll?' could elicit different answers.

In the activity you have just done, the answers are: there are eight ways to dress the dolls. Cindy can be dressed in each outfit and so can Barbie. Each doll can be dressed in four different ways.

The first gives you the pattern

1 doll	2 outfits	4 ways
2 dolls		8 ways
3 dolls		12 ways
4 dolls		16 ways

whereas the second gives you

2 outfits	4 ways
3 outfits	9 ways
4 outfits	16 ways

Developments

Whichever path you choose, try to encourage the pupils to explain to each other what is happening and why they know they have dressed each doll in all the possible combinations.

The nature of this activity would make the beginning of it appropriate for young pupils.

Older pupils may be able to **PREDICT** the number of ways with 5 dolls and to **TEST** their prediction. It is not likely that they will **GENERALISE** (see a connection between the number of dolls and the number of ways of dressing them or the number of items of clothing and the number of ways). It is worth gently exploring – children never cease to destroy our expectations! If you were working with older pupils, they may well see the connection.

You can, of course, ask a series of simple questions such as:
'What is the difference between the number of outfits?'
'How many outfits altogether?'
'What do we call these numbers?' (even)
'Do we ever get an odd number for an answer?' etc. etc.

National Curriculum Targets

Attainment Target 1: Levels 1, 2, 3
Attainment Target 2: Level 1
Attainment Target 3: Levels 1, 2, 3
Attainment Target 5: Level 3

Nuffield Scheme Cross-reference

Nuffield Maths 2 Teachers' Handbook   N11

STARTER 3: Traffic Jams

You need:

Four cars in different colours;
a road mat or equivalent;
copies of Sheets 3A and 3B on pages 40–41.

Organisation

In the same way as dolls were dressed in different outfits, cars can be placed in traffic jams.

Once again this is a suitable activity for the teacher to introduce informally to any size group. Ideally, it is done by placing toy cars on a roadway but can be simulated using cubes or by colouring, cutting and sticking *Worksheet 3*.

The basic idea

It is perhaps best to start with two cars. They could be placed red car, blue car or blue car, red car. There are two ways that the cars can be in a traffic jam.

Three cars could be placed:
red yellow blue
yellow blue red
red blue yellow
blue yellow red
blue red yellow
yellow red blue.
Each car can be in each position twice; once with another colour car in front of it and then with that colour car behind it.

Four cars will generate 24 jams which teachers may feel is too large a number for young children.

Developments

Simple questions could include:
'Which car is first this time?'
'Which car is in between the red car and the blue car?'
'Which car is the red car in front of?'

You may not wish to explore the number relationships but you will no doubt have noticed that it increases to a pattern that multiplies the number of cars by the number of jams with one less car. This is because each new car can be put next to each car in the previous jam.

National Curriculum Targets

Attainment Target 1:   Levels 1, 2, 3
Attainment Target 5:   Level 1
Attainment Target 11: Level 1
Attainment Target 13: Level 1

Nuffield Scheme Cross-reference

Nuffield Maths 1 Teachers' Handbook   N4
Nuffield Maths 2 Teachers' Handbook   N11

STARTER 4: Dice

You need:

Three large sponge dice;
copies of Sheet 4 on page 42.

Organisation

This is another idea that works well as a teacher-led informal session. Initially, you can hold the dice yourself but there are advantages to using weaker pupils for this task as they can gain practice in counting whilst contributing to a class activity.

At some point you may wish to give individual/pairs or a small group of pupils their own dice with which to **INVESTIGATE**. At any point the pupils can record on the Worksheet 4 or in their own way.

The basic idea

Briefly check that pupils recognise the values of the dot arrays on the dice. Simple questions could include: 'If I can see 5 what can you see?' or 'If 3 is on the top what is on the bottom?' (Opposite faces of the die add up to 7.)

Holding up two dice, ask what score you have. Repeat this for several combinations.
What scores can you make?
What scores can you not make?
Can the children explain why?
Now reverse the question. 'If I want to score 7, how could I do it?' If you are looking at two dice, there are six 'different answers'. We know that 2 + 5 gives the same total as 5 + 2, but not all the pupils will be at this stage and if you are using different coloured dice, the difference is obvious.

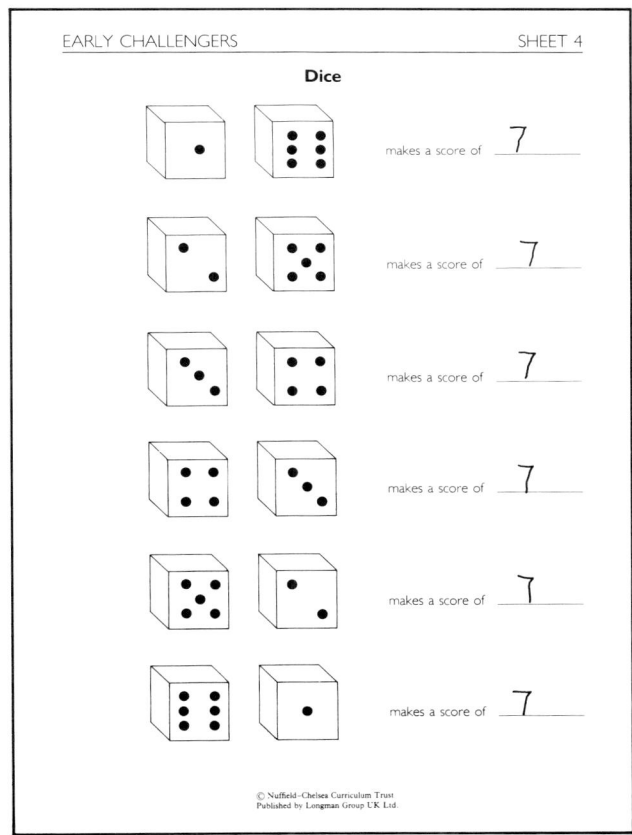

You can now ask a pattern search question. 'How many different ways can I make each possible score?'

The pupils will find that:

— you can make 2 one way
— you can make 3 two ways
— you can make 4 three ways
— you can make 5 four ways.

They may now be able to **PREDICT**.

They can **TEST** their prediction. They will find that you can make 6 in five ways and they already know that you can make 7 in six ways.

They may well be able to **GENERALISE** (look for a connection between the number you are trying to score and the number of ways of scoring it). In this case, it is very simple but does give an idea of the process.

Developments

Time to ask a '**WHAT IF?**' question. Suggestions will include using more dice. The children may have seen dice other than six-sided ones and suggest using these.

You can extend the activity by pretending to stick the dice together to form cuboidal dice and investigate the scores you can achieve. Does this depend on what faces you stick together?

National Curriculum Targets

Attainment Target 1: Levels 1, 2, 3
Attainment Target 2: Level 1
Attainment Target 3: Levels 1, 2, 3
Attainment Target 5: Levels 2, 3
Attainment Target 13: Level 1

Nuffield Scheme Cross-reference

Nuffield Maths 1 Teachers' Handbook   N3, N5, N6
Nuffield Maths 2 Teachers' Handbook   N9

STARTER 5: Make Five

You need:

Your usual rod number apparatus e.g. Cuisenaire, Colour Factor or Stern; copies of Sheets 5, 5A, 5B, 5C, 5D or 5E from pages 43–48.

Organisation

This is best done by individuals or pairs in the first instance although the activity could develop into a longer-term larger group activity.

The basic idea

The pupils are asked to find as many different ways of matching a representation of five as they can.

You may wish to leave this totally open or to break the task up into smaller units, e.g. using a maximum of two different colour rods.
The pupils can record each matching on Worksheet 5 using crayons.
The pupils can be asked to write the number sentence for each representation underneath each picture.

They can also use any of the other worksheets – 5A, 5B, 5C, 5D or 5E – to record the ways of making 5.

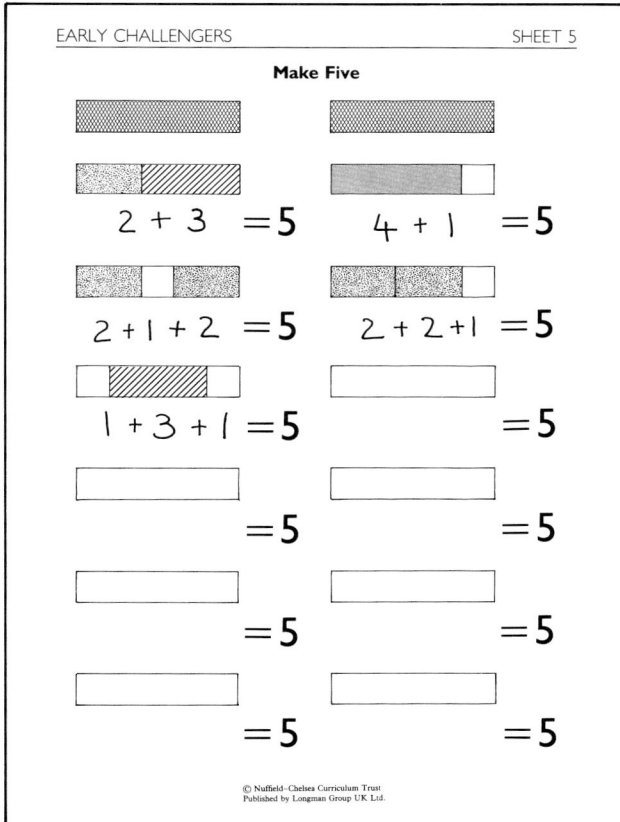

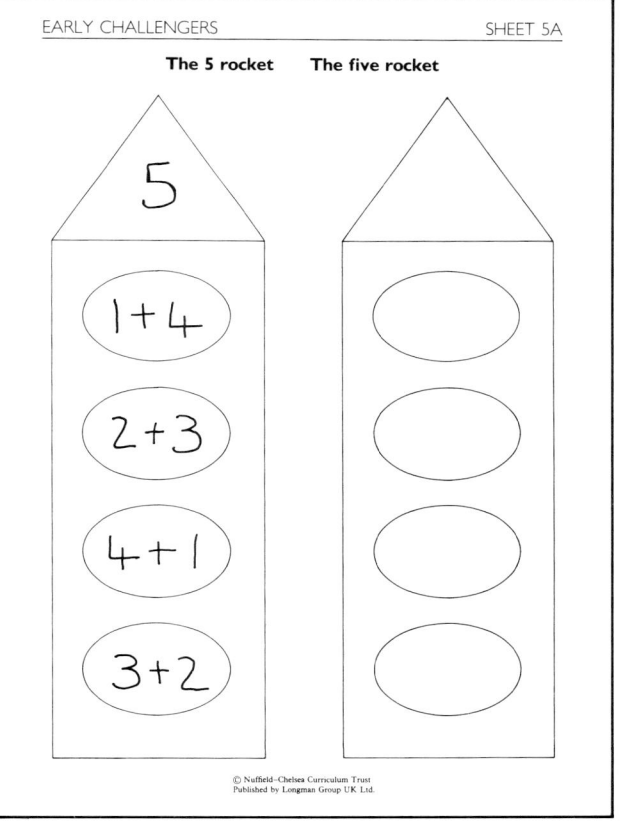

The 5 Star   The five Star

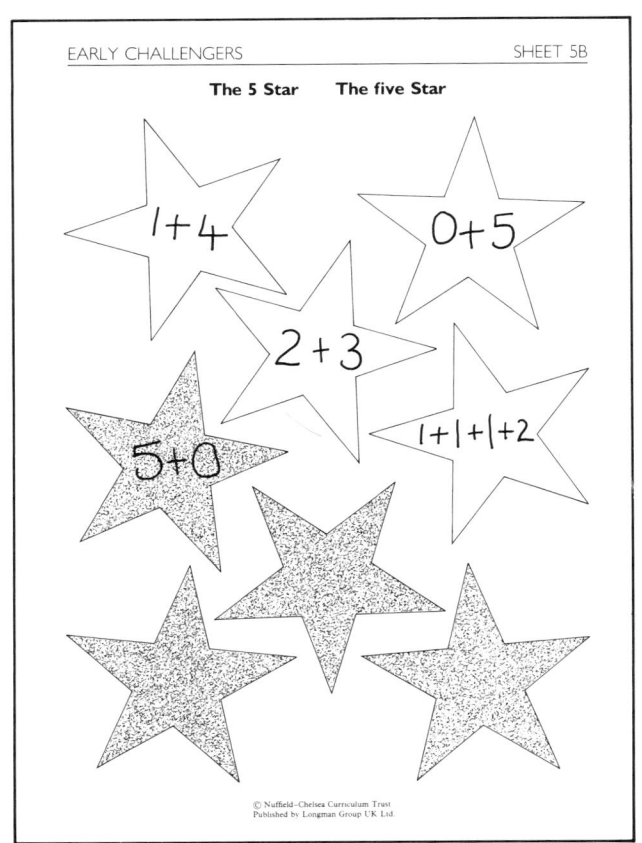

The 5 train   The five train

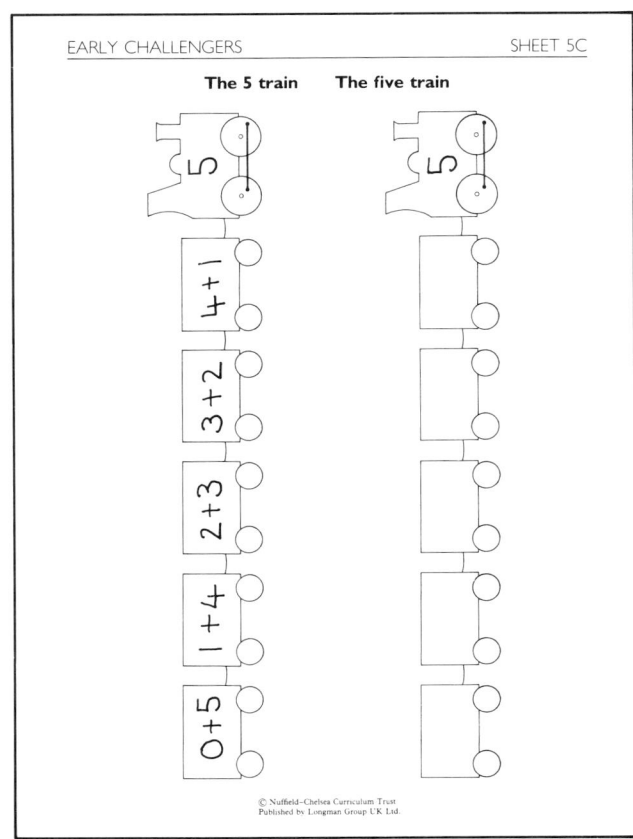

The 5 cat   The five cat

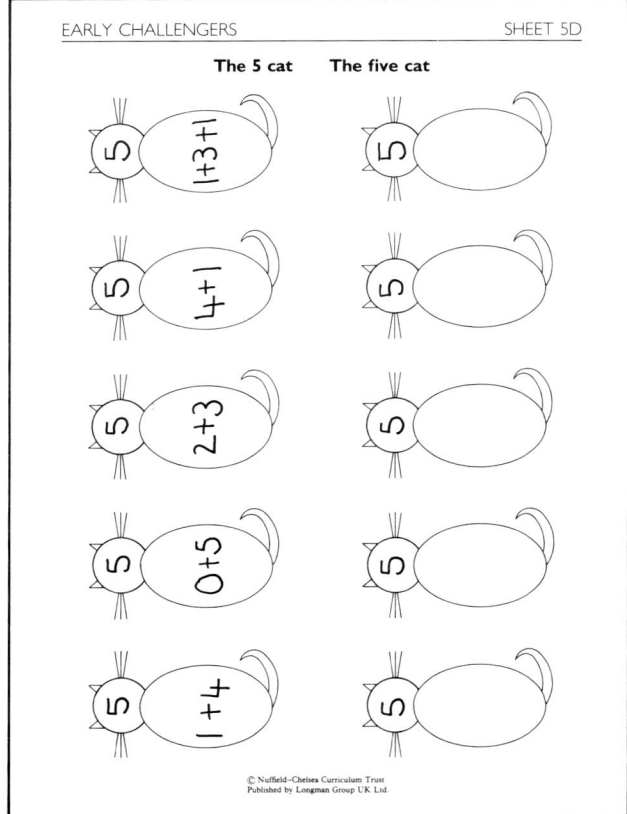

The 5 fish   The five fish

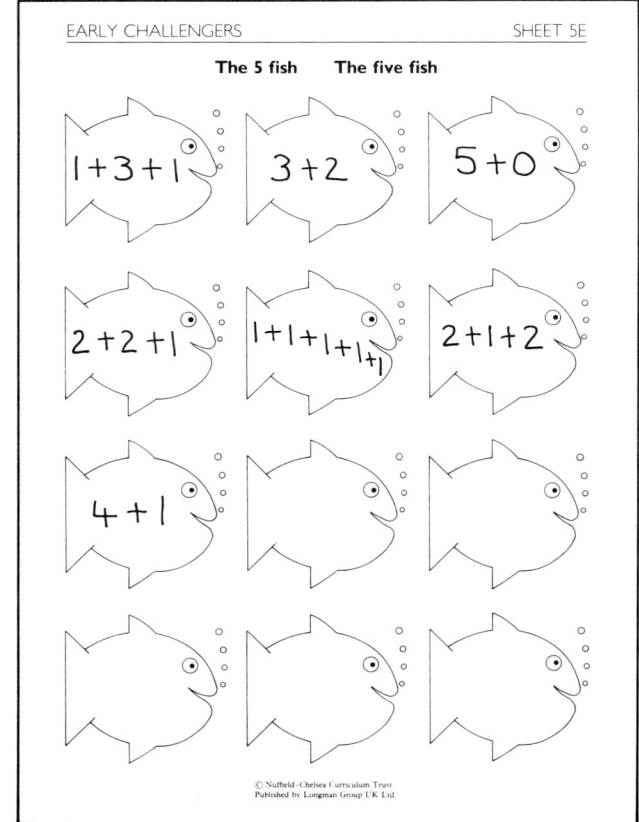

Developments

All of the above 'Basic ideas' involved addition. A possible suggestion from a 'WHAT IF?' question would involve the flexibility to use any operation. Answers could be recorded on any of the sheets.

The initial activity could be repeated using different starting numbers. You may wish the pupils to use calculators or to work in the abstract.

WARNING: Do not look for a relationship or pattern in the different number of ways of making a number with addition. To say it is very complicated is an understatement. If you are interested, find out more about the Indian mathematician Ramanujin who worked at Cambridge during the 1920s and 1930s. If you limit it to combinations of two numbers, then it is simple.

You can make 1 in 2 ways.
You can make 2 in 3 ways.
You can make 3 in 4 ways.   If the use of 0 is allowed
You can make 4 in 5 ways. $(0 + 1, 1 + 0; 0 + 2, 2 + 0, 1 + 1;$
You can make 5 in 6 ways.   and so on).

The pupils can now PREDICT and TEST their prediction. This connects with Starter 4: Dice.

They will find that you can make 6 in seven ways.
It is also very simple to GENERALISE (find a connection between the number you are making and the number of ways of making it).
If you do not wish to use 0, there is still a simple pattern:
You make 2 in 1 way
You make 3 in 2 ways
You make 4 in 3 ways . . .

National Curriculum Targets

Attainment Target 1:   Levels 1, 2, 3
Attainment Target 2:   Level 1
Attainment Target 3:   Levels 1, 2, 3
Attainment Target 5:   Levels 2, 3
Attainment Target 8:   Level 1
Attainment Target 13: Level 1

Nuffield Scheme Cross-reference

Nuffield Maths 1 Teachers' Handbook   N2, N3, N5, N6
Nuffield Maths 2 Teachers' Handbook   N7, N11

STARTER 6: Making Numbers (Limited Entry)

You need:

A basic calculator for each pupil;
copies of Sheet 6 on page 49.

Organisation

Lends itself to individual, pair, small or large group activity – depending on your needs.

The basic idea

Some of the keys on the calculator do not work. Can you make a target answer using only the working keys?
Perhaps start with a mixture of number and operation keys working.
For example, can you make all the numbers from 1 to 20 if only these keys work?

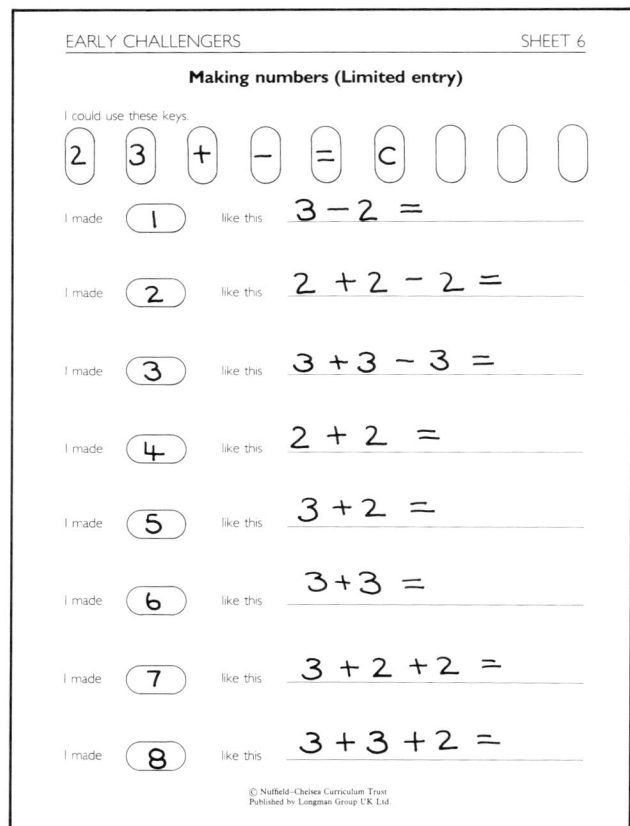

Then you might try something like,
'What numbers can you make if only these keys work?'

Developments

There are few limits to the developments. This could, of course, stretch very able pupils of all ages way beyond the primary school, particularly if more complicated operations were available. This lends itself to discussion between pupils of how they tackled the problem.

Written work can be very interesting. The teacher can learn much to assist in the assessment of pupils, particularly about their true competency with calculations and their understanding of the four rules.

National Curriculum Targets

Attainment Target 1: Levels 1, 2, 3
Attainment Target 3: Levels 2, 3, 4 . . .
Attainment Target 5: Levels 2, 3

Nuffield Scheme Cross-reference

Nuffield Maths 1 Teachers' Handbook   N6
Nuffield Maths 2 Teachers' Handbook   N7, N9, N10, N11, N12

STARTER 7: Magic Arithmegons

You need:

Game card (on page 53) and the set of digit cards (on page 54);
copies of Sheet 7 on page 50.

Organisation

This can be done by individuals, pairs or larger groups, depending on
preferences. Some pupils find it very irritating to be working on a problem
and have someone else solve it just as the penny is about to drop. You can
collect different solutions and different observations from individuals to
build this into a group activity.

The basic idea

The pupils have to place the numbers 1 2 3 4 5 6 into the boxes so that
the sum of each side of the triangle is the same.
There is not one solution only; it is possible to arrange the numbers to
achieve totals of 9, 10, 11 and 12.

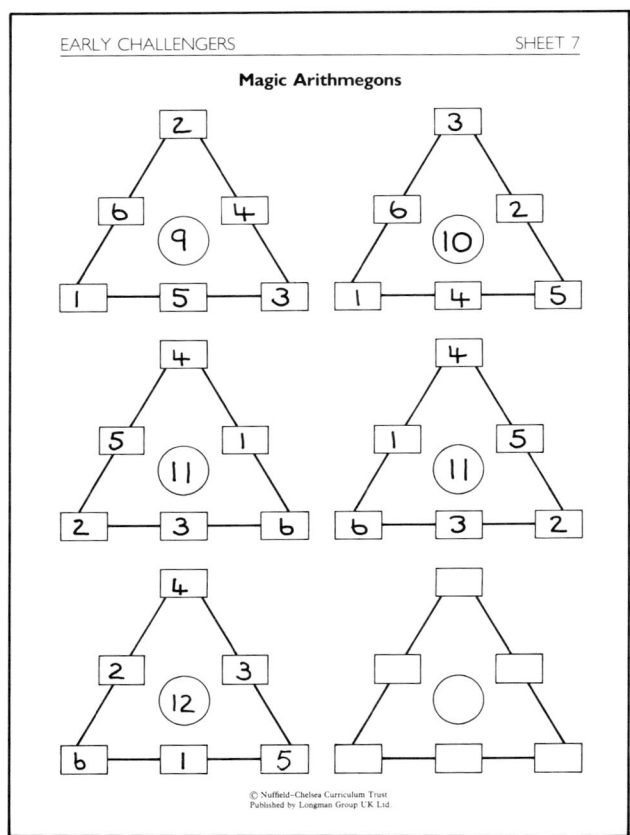

Each solution is unique; apparent variations being merely rotations or
reflections of each other.

If you examine the solutions, you will find interesting patterns in the way that
the numbers are placed. The corners of each solution allow the pupils to
GENERALISE so that, given any six consecutive numbers, they can very
quickly create solutions.

They may also be able to explain to you why 9 is the smallest solution and 12
the largest.

Developments

BEWARE! It is very tempting to develop this so that the pupils are given, say, four-, five-sided figures etc. and more numbers. In fact, since developing this idea I have seen it used in several sources.

The 'rule' learnt in the triangle solution does not help solve a rectangle problem, in fact it is little use and could hinder.

The five-sided figure would be the one to try next, but the pattern of solution begins to become more complex and can tax lively adult mathematical minds! Colleagues have articles of a mathematical nature in production as I write.

National Curriculum Targets

Attainment Target 3: Levels 2, 3
Attainment Target 5: Levels 2, 3

Nuffield Scheme Cross-reference

Nuffield Maths 1 Teachers' Handbook N6
Nuffield Maths 2 Teachers' Handbook N8

STARTER 8: Polyominoes

You need:

Interlocking squares such as Clixi or Polydron; *or* card squares of side about 5 cm;
copies of Sheet 8 on page 51.

Organisation

Ideal for pairs or small groups but can be appropriate for individuals or large groups.

The basic idea

Take three squares of the same size and fit them together flat on the table. This can be interpreted in several ways. What is intended is that the squares are joined along a **complete edge** without overlapping. Is it possible to follow the rules but fit the squares together in different ways? You may well need to negotiate what is meant by 'different'. Children are often much more rigorous than adults and do not allow rotations or reflections. The solutions discussed here work to the rules quoted above.
If your groups choose other rules, you will allow more solutions.

It is possible to fit three squares together in two ways (diagram A). These arrangements can be recorded using sticky paper on squared paper, or on Sheet 8.

Now add a fourth square. How many ways can these be joined? Once again the results can be recorded. This time there should be five different arrangements (diagram B).
It can be rewarding to ask pupils to describe each of their solutions to each other without the use of diagrams or waving hands.

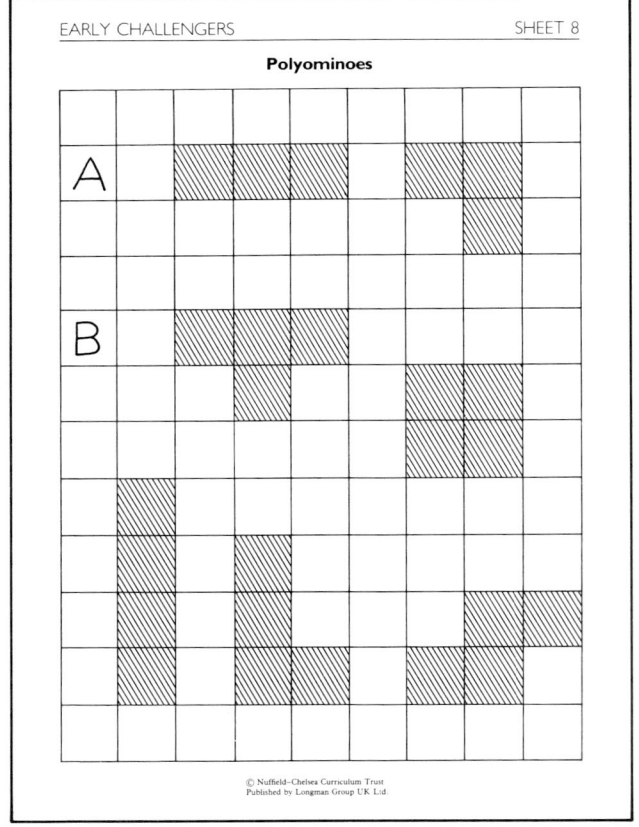

Developments

Continue to increase the number of squares. (The number of possible solutions increases significantly – a fuller treatment of *Polyominoes* is given in Chapter 10 of *Nuffield Maths 6 Teachers' Handbook*.)

With 5 squares, do any of the arrangements fold up to make an open box?
With 6 squares, do any of the arrangements fold up to make a cube?
Is the perimeter (distance round the outside) of each shape made with the same number of squares always the same?
Take each solution in turn and use two colours to shade it in.
'How many ways can this be done?'
'WHAT IF? you use three or four colours?'
'Are any of the shapes symmetrical?'
'Do any of the solutions fit together?'
'What shapes do they make?'
Instead of squares, use cubes. (See *Starter 9*.)

National Curriculum Targets

Attainment Target 9:   Levels 1, 2
Attainment Target 11: Levels 1, 2, 3

Nuffield Scheme Cross-reference

Nuffield Maths 2 Teachers' Handbook   S2

STARTER 9: Multilink

You need:

A selection of interlocking cubes (such as Multilink) for each pupil.

Organisation

This works particularly well as a whole class, long-term activity to which the pupils can contribute as an ongoing task. The teacher can introduce it informally and use the build-up structure as in towers to move from individual to pair, to group task.

The basic idea

This is the three-dimensional version of the previous activity.
Pupils are asked to join a given number of interlocking cubes together in as many different ways as possible.

To limit the activity to a manageable task you should use only one colour cube per pupil to focus on the difference in shape rather than the difference in colour position.

Developments

As before you can concentrate on tessellation symmetry rather than number patterns. You could also discuss cubes that can be seen and cubes that cannot be seen.
'How many cubes have been used altogether?'
'Count the outside faces. Are these the same for each version using the same number of cubes?'

National Curriculum Targets

Attainment Target 9: Levels 1, 2
Attainment Target 11: Levels 1, 2, 3

Nuffield Scheme Cross-reference

Nuffield Maths 1 Teachers' Handbook S1
Nuffield Maths 2 Teachers' Handbook S2

STARTER 10: Necklace

You need:

Large wooden beads in different colours and/or shapes and/or sizes.

Organisation

Best done by individuals but they can be in a small group all working on different examples.

The basic idea

A very simple basic idea in which the pupils are asked to reproduce a short snake or necklace made of beads. They would be copying an actual necklace rather than a representation and would not be choosing from a large, random selection of beads but a carefully chosen, small selection.

Sometimes only provide the correct colour shape and size of bead; on other occasions include 'interference' beads of the correct colour and shape but wrong size, etc.

Developments

One pupil can be asked to describe the necklace that is hidden from the rest and it must be made from the description.
Pupils must ask questions of the necklace holder to find out how to make it.

National Curriculum Targets

Attainment Target 1: Level 1
Attainment Target 5: Level 1
Attainment Target 8: Level 1
Attainment Target 9: Level 1
Attainment Target 10: Levels 1, 2, 3
Attainment Target 11: Level 1

Nuffield Scheme Cross-reference

Nuffield Maths 1 Teachers' Handbook   N2, N3, N4

STARTER 11: Carpet Tiles

You need:

Old square carpet or lino tiles *or* squares of stiff card (perhaps covered in plastic film) of side minimum 30 cm; large floor space.

Organisation

Works well with a large group as well as smaller groups co-operating to complete a design.

The basic idea

Any design made from squares can be created.
Simple designs could be lines repeating a colour pattern.
Starter 8: Polyominoes could be done in this medium.

A pattern made by starting from one square and adding squares to a rule such as they must touch on one side only (diagram A).

A triangular arrangement made by increasing the next row by a given number of squares (diagrams B and C), could lead to much discussion, description, prediction etc.

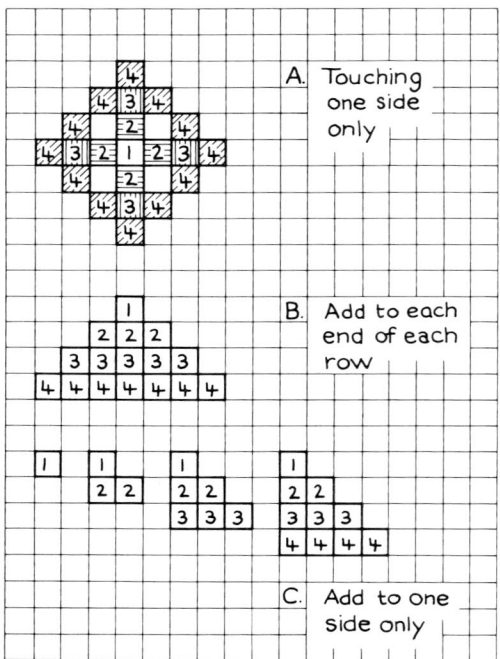

Developments

The shape of the tiles could be changed to triangles, hexagons, etc. The size of the tiles could be varied to allow more simple patterns.

National Curriculum Targets

Attainment Target 10: Level 2
Attainment Target 11: Level 1

Nuffield Scheme Cross-reference

Nuffield Maths 1 Teachers' Handbook S1
Nuffield Maths 2 Teachers' Handbook S2

STARTER 12: Number Square to Number Line

You need:

As for *Starter 11* but with consecutive numbers from 1 onwards written on one side of each tile.

Organisation

As for *Starter 11*.

The basic idea

The numbers can be placed into the usual number line arrangement.
Pupils can be asked to stand on tiles to a number pattern e.g. odds, evens, five times table etc.

Tiles can be turned over to make different number patterns. The teacher can turn tiles over and ask the pupils what rule has been used to turn them over.

A tile for zero can be introduced.

The line can be rearranged into a square to explain that arrangement.
The above activities can be repeated to describe the new pattern created.

Developments

The number square can be arranged as a non-standard format, e.g. 1 in the bottom left; as a spiral; etc.

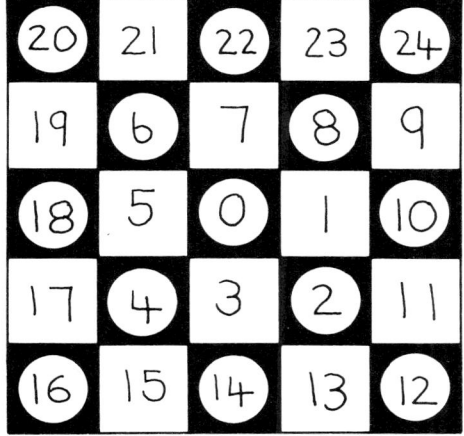

National Curriculum Targets

Attainment Target 2: Levels 1, 2
Attainment Target 5: Levels 1, 3

Nuffield Scheme Cross-reference

Nuffield Maths 1 Teachers' Handbook   N4, N6
Nuffield Maths 2 Teachers' Handbook   N7, N9, N10

STARTER 13: Wheels

You need:

Various items with very different wheel sizes: e.g. golf trolley, shopping trolley, toddler's bicycle, toy cars, doll's pram;
long corridor or other space to allow a measured distance of at least 5 metres.

Organisation

The initial introduction can be done with the whole class. The experimental work can be allocated as appropriate; pairs work particularly well with a single piece of apparatus.

The basic idea

Show the group two items: one with larger wheels, the other with smaller wheels in motion. Pose questions about the wheels, including. 'Do the wheels go round the same amount?'

The pupils usually respond with a mixture of the three possible answers: 'Yes', 'No', 'I don't know'.

Ask them how they could find out?
It is very important that you do not push them towards the experiment you have in mind.

You need to make supportive responses and allow groups or individuals to suggest and develop **FAIR TESTS** that will demonstrate that over a given distance, the smaller the wheel the more times it will revolve.

This is, of course, the principle behind the trundle wheel which is used in many classrooms and remains a mystery to many pupils! To show a marked difference, the wheels should be markedly different in size and the distance should be as long as practicality allows. A corridor is probably better than a classroom.

Developments

The developments probably would lie in the sophistication of the system used to count the wheel turns. Simply, this could be a child counting every time a chalk mark passes a marked point on the axle.

With pupils becoming more technologically minded it is inappropriate to limit expectations.

One class of middle infants became interested in the speed of the wheel and discussed that concept at great length.

National Curriculum Targets

This activity would also help to achieve targets within the Science Curriculum.
Attainment Target 8: Levels 1, 2, 3
Attainment Target 9: Levels 1, 2, 3
Attainment Target 11: Level 1

Nuffield Scheme Cross-reference

Nuffield Maths 1 Teachers' Handbook   T1, L1
Nuffield Maths 2 Teachers' Handbook   T2, L2

STARTER 14: Noah's Ark

You need:

Toy animals or animal masks *or* copies of Sheet 14 on page 52;
cubes or counters to represent each type of animal.

Organisation

A good class lesson – plenty of scope for all to take part and for the teacher to
ask questions according to the pupil's ability.
Can be tied up with art/craft and drama.
Makes a good assembly idea based on a Bible story and the '**WHAT IF?**'
questions.

The basic idea

Quite simply take the basic Noah's Ark story and explore '**WHAT IF?**' the
animals had gone in 3 by 3 or 4 by 4.

Children can represent the animals and with different numbers of species
count or calculate total number of animals entering the Ark.
Concrete materials can be used to represent each situation.

Developments

Traffic Jams with animals! See *Starter 3*.

Wall displays of table facts built up of animals entering the Ark. Drama.
Assembly. Song: 'The Animals Went in N by N'.

National Curriculum Targets

Attainment Target 1: Levels 1, 2, 3
Attainment Target 2: Levels 1, 2, 3
Attainment Target 3: Levels 3, 4

Nuffield Scheme Cross-reference

Nuffield Maths 1 Teachers' Handbook   N1, N2, N3, N4
Nuffield Maths 2 Teachers' Handbook   N11

STARTER 15: Money

You need:

Coins of the realm *or* representations.

Organisation

This activity lends itself to individual or co-operative work and the various target sums could be set to different groups according to their ability.

The basic idea

Given a sum of money to make from the coins of the realm, how many different ways can you make that total?

The coins available can be limited to control the number of variations. The work has to be done very systematically to check that all possible solutions have been found and that a solution is not repeated. The activity encourages the pupils to try different forms of recording – so no recording sheet is included in this pack.

Two methods of recording often developed by pupils are illustrated below. It is important that any method employed is pupil developed and not teacher imposed.

1p	2p	5p	10p	
6	2	1		15p
13	1			15p
	5	1		15p
2	4	1		15p

10p 5p 1p = 16p

10p 2p 2p 2p = 16p

10p 2p 1p 1p 1p 1p = 16p

Developments

You might consider looking for a relationship between the number of solutions possible and the sum being made. This is not as straightforward as you might expect if you have tried *Starter 5*.

There are further complications as the number of coins available for use increases and as the sum you are trying to make gets larger.
There are interesting variations to consider along the lines; if I am not sure of the bus fare but I know that it could be 35p, 40p or 50p, what would be the best coins to have ready to pay the driver?
What would be the minimum number of coins I could have to be sure that I could pay any of the sums and what would those coins be?

National Curriculum Targets

Attainment Target 3: Levels 1, 2, 3
Attainment Target 8: Level 2

Nuffield Scheme Cross-reference

Nuffield Maths 1 Teachers' Handbook   M1
Nuffield Maths 2 Teachers' Handbook   M2

STARTER 16: What Coin?

You need:

Coins of the realm *or* representations.

The basic idea

One pupil describes a coin, one attribute at a time, e.g. 'It is bronze', and the other pupil has to suggest what that coin might be.

Developments

The pupil who is trying to identify the coin asks questions to which the answer may only be 'yes' or 'no'.

The coin is held behind the back and the pupil describes the coin by what can be felt.

National Curriculum Target

Attainment Target 8: Level 2

Nuffield Scheme Cross-reference

Nuffield Maths 1 Teachers' Handbook   M1
Nuffield Maths 2 Teachers' Handbook   M2

STARTER 17: Weighing

You need:

Boxes for each group of children containing five items of differing weights. Fabric bags can be filled with straw, foam chips etc. to make lighter objects. Tins from the cupboard or old weights will provide heavier items. Try to include smaller, heavier items and larger, lighter ones.

The basic idea

The items in each box have to be ordered by weight. The way the pupils do this can be varied according to which skill you wish them to develop: e.g. by feel; using balancing; using balancing and weights; using calibrated scales.

Each group records their order in their own way and describes how they tackled the task.

Over a period of time – a lesson, a day, a week – all groups order the items in each box. At the end of that period of time a teacher-led lesson compares the results and the methods used.

The use of the board to build up tabulated results is useful and demonstrates exactly how a table of results displays a group of findings. This can then lead to much less confusion when the pupils are faced with teacher or scheme produced tables. It is particularly important that the pupils use their own recording system initially; so there is no record sheet included in the pack.

Developments

This could be repeated with different measuring skills, e.g. capacity of bottles.

National Curriculum Targets

Attainment Target 8: Levels 1, 2, 3

Nuffield Scheme Cross-reference

Nuffield Maths 1 Teachers' Handbook W1
Nuffield Maths 2 Teachers' Handbook W2

STARTER 18: Pathways

You need:

A blindfold;
large boxes, e.g. from household items such as televisions, vacuum cleaners, computers;
Bigtrak or equivalent (if available).

Organisation

Can be set up by a group and tried by other groups, individuals or pairs. Can be started by individual or pair and developed to include more people.

The basic idea

A maze is built around which a blindfolded pupil has to be directed by other pupils. The instructions can be recorded and used by another group to direct a different blindfolded pupil around the maze. The language that may be used in the directions can be limited, e.g. must be more precise than 'keep going', 'stop', 'a little bit more', 'turn the other way'.

A Bigtrak or similar toy can be programmed to move round the maze.

Developments

Directions to parts of the school can be devised for visitors to find their way about.

Use of LOGO and a floor turtle with various mazes.

National Curriculum Targets

Attainment Target 11: Levels 1, 2, 3

Nuffield Scheme Cross-reference

Bronto Book: *Left, right*

STARTER 19: Think of a Block

You need:

Set of logiblocs or other structured sorting material, or small sub-set (depending on the ability of the group).

Organisation

A good small group activity that can work well with low teacher intervention once the basic idea is clear.

The basic idea

One of the group is the THINKER and chooses a piece from the set. The piece is not removed or indicated in any way. The rest of the group must identify it by asking questions that require a 'yes' or 'no' answer.

Developments

Can the guessers identify the piece in a minimum number of moves?
Are some questions better than others to ask?
Does luck play a part?

National Curriculum Targets

Attainment Target 10: Levels 1, 2, 3

Nuffield Scheme Cross-reference

Nuffield Maths 1 Teachers' Handbook   S1
Nuffield Maths 2 Teachers' Handbook   S2

STARTER 20: Recording Ideas

You need:

Sandcastles made from plasticine or modelling clay;
flag sticks e.g. lollipop sticks or tomato canes.

Organisation

This activity allows a large group to build up a pictorial representation of
data. It lends itself to being done with the whole class through an informal,
teacher-led discussion.

The basic idea

Often teachers will form pupils into sets according to an attribute, e.g. colour
of sweater. Each pupil is given a flag and asked to colour it in the appropriate
way. Sandcastles are made from plasticine of corresponding colours and
pupils are invited to put their flag in the appropriate sandcastle.
All the usual sorts of questions associated with the work can ensue.

Developments

Variations would include flowers in vases.
The pupils could be asked to place an appropriately coloured Unifix cube
next to the sandcastle and these could be fixed together to form a
three-dimensional block graph.

National Curriculum Targets

Attainment Target 12: Levels 1, 2
Attainment Target 13: Level 1

Nuffield Scheme Cross-reference

Nuffield Maths 1 Teachers' Handbook   N4

Towers 3 cubes high

Towers 2 cubes high

Towers 1 cube high

Towers 4 cubes high

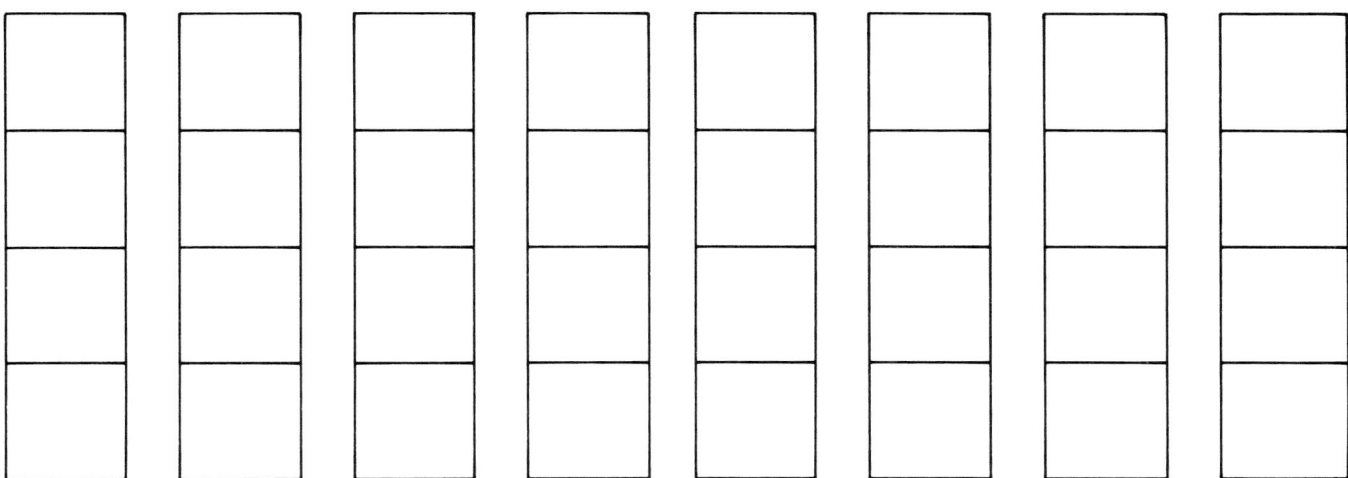

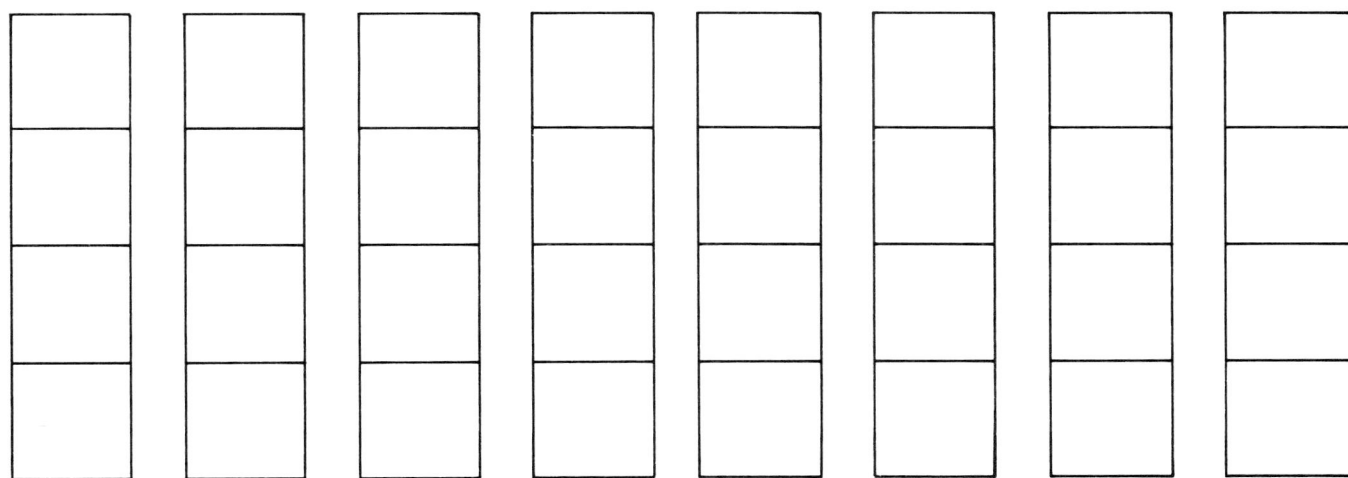

Dolls

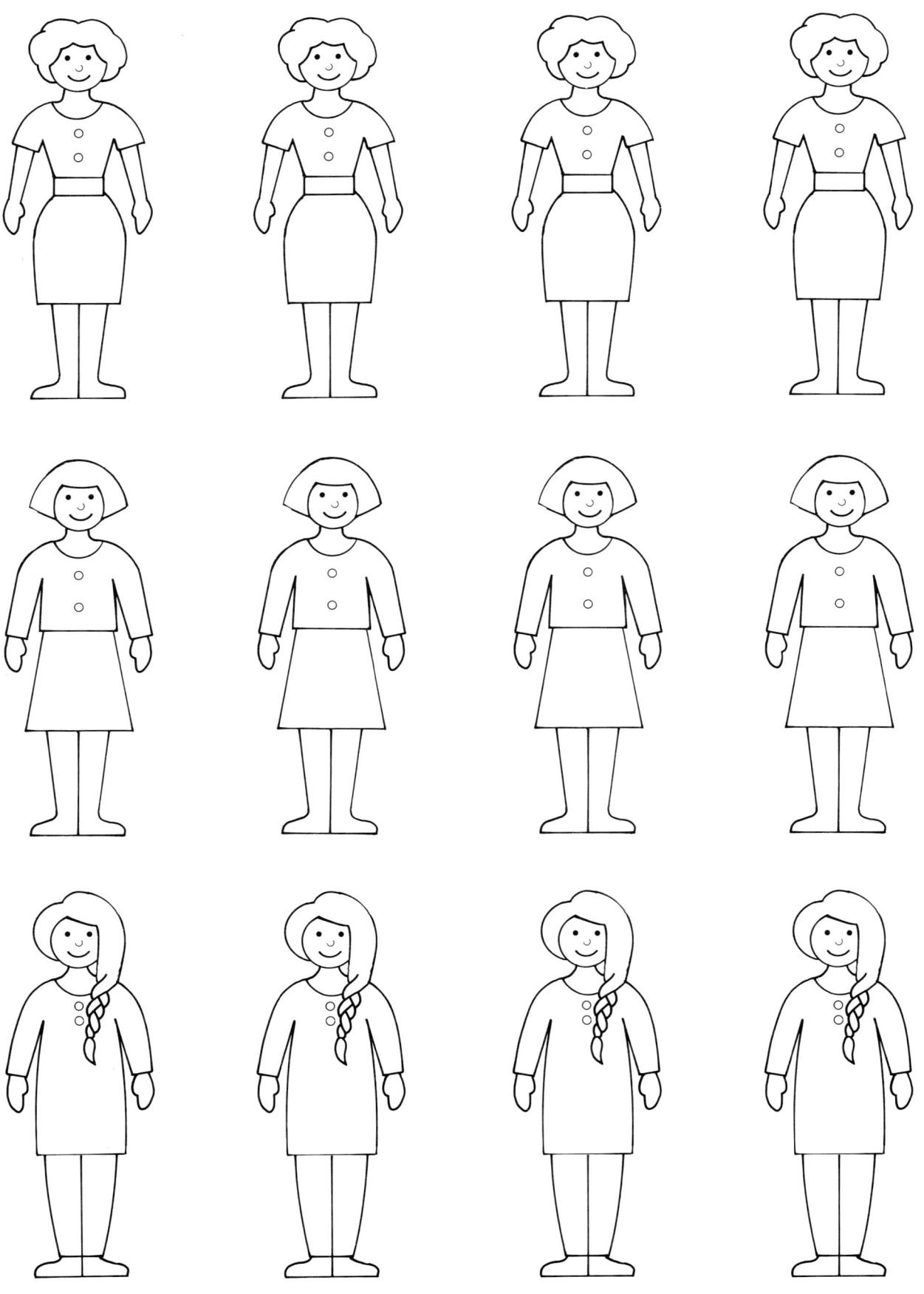

Traffic Jams (2 cars)

Cars to cut and stick

Traffic Jams (3 cars)

Traffic Jams (4 cars)

Dice

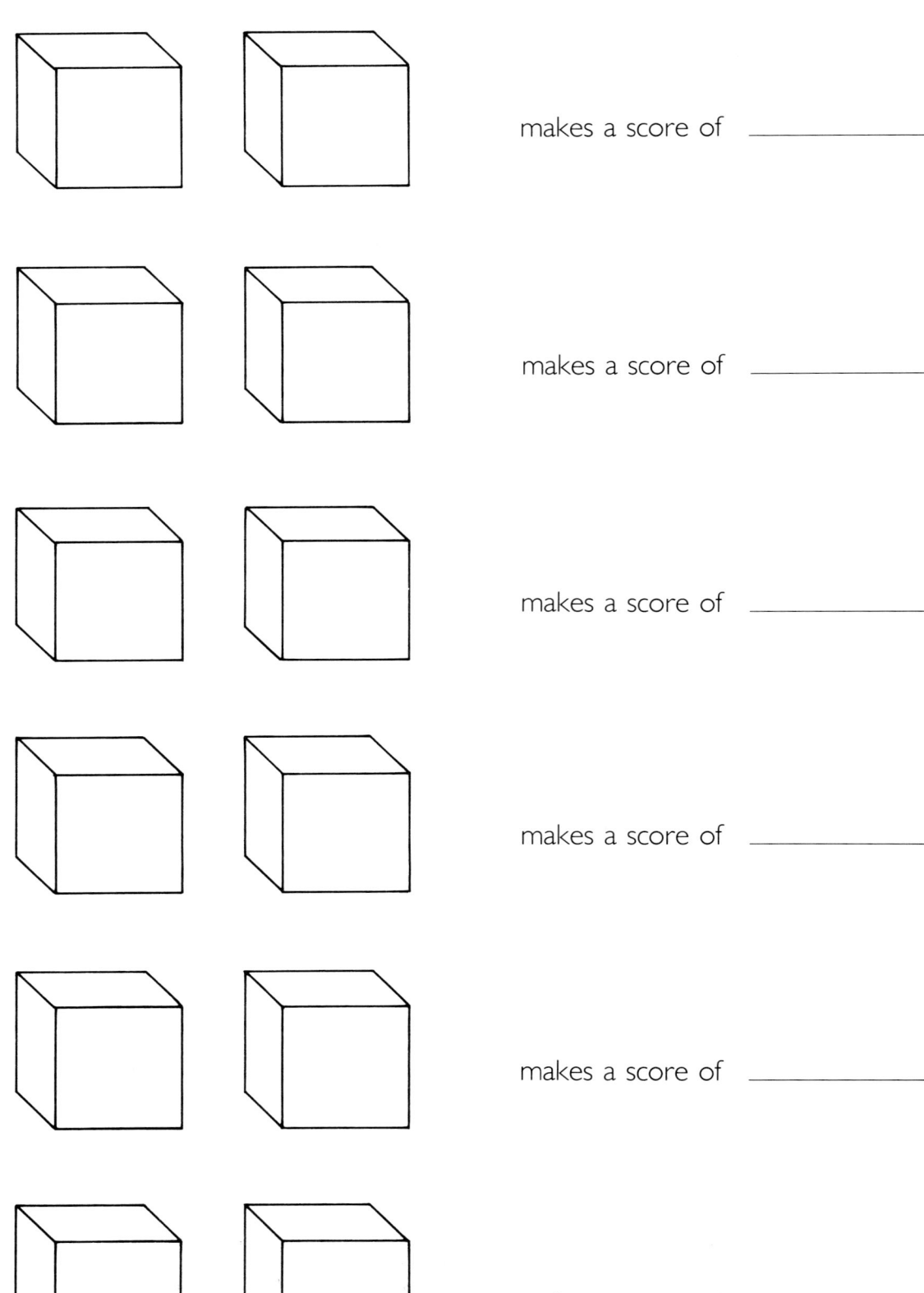

makes a score of _____

makes a score of _____

makes a score of _____

makes a score of _____

makes a score of _____

makes a score of _____

Make Five

$=5$

$=5$

$=5$

$=5$

$=5$

$=5$

$=5$

$=5$

$=5$

$=5$

$=5$

$=5$

The 5 rocket   The five rocket

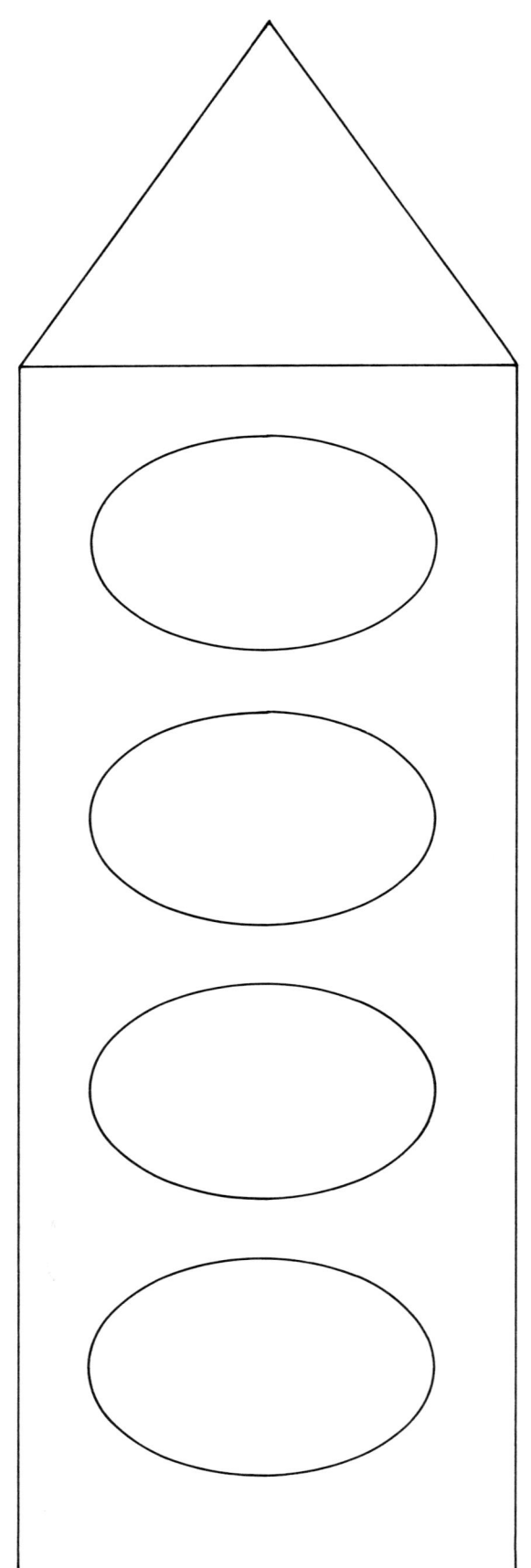
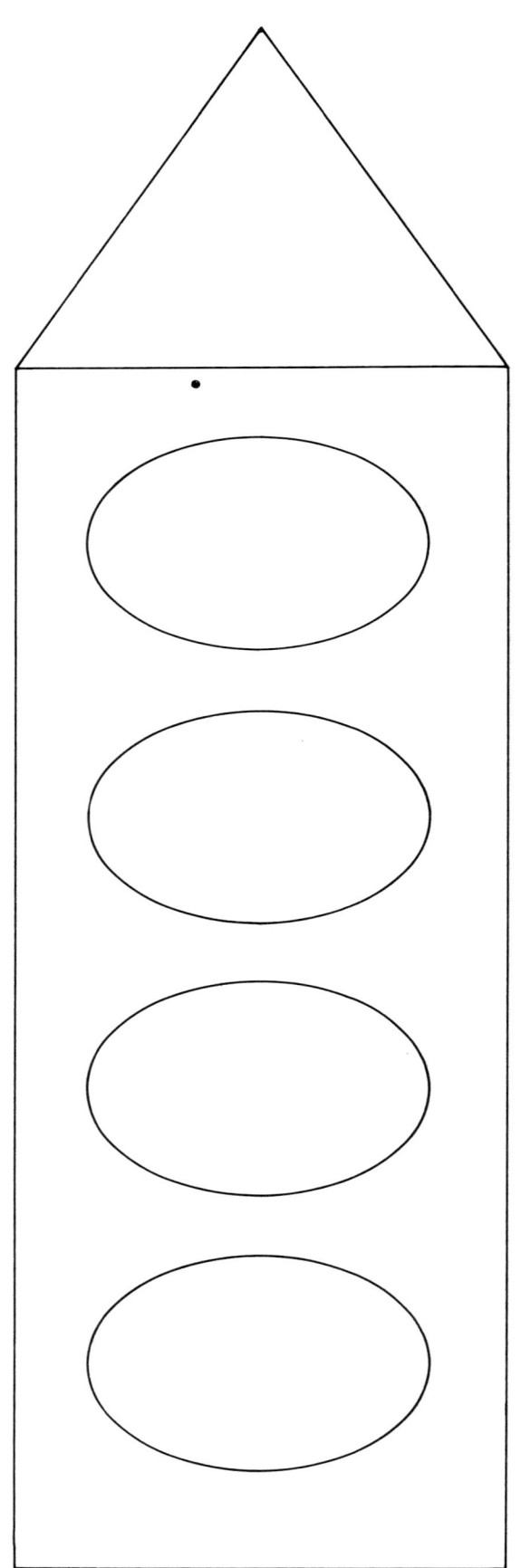

The 5 Star   The five Star

The 5 train   The five train

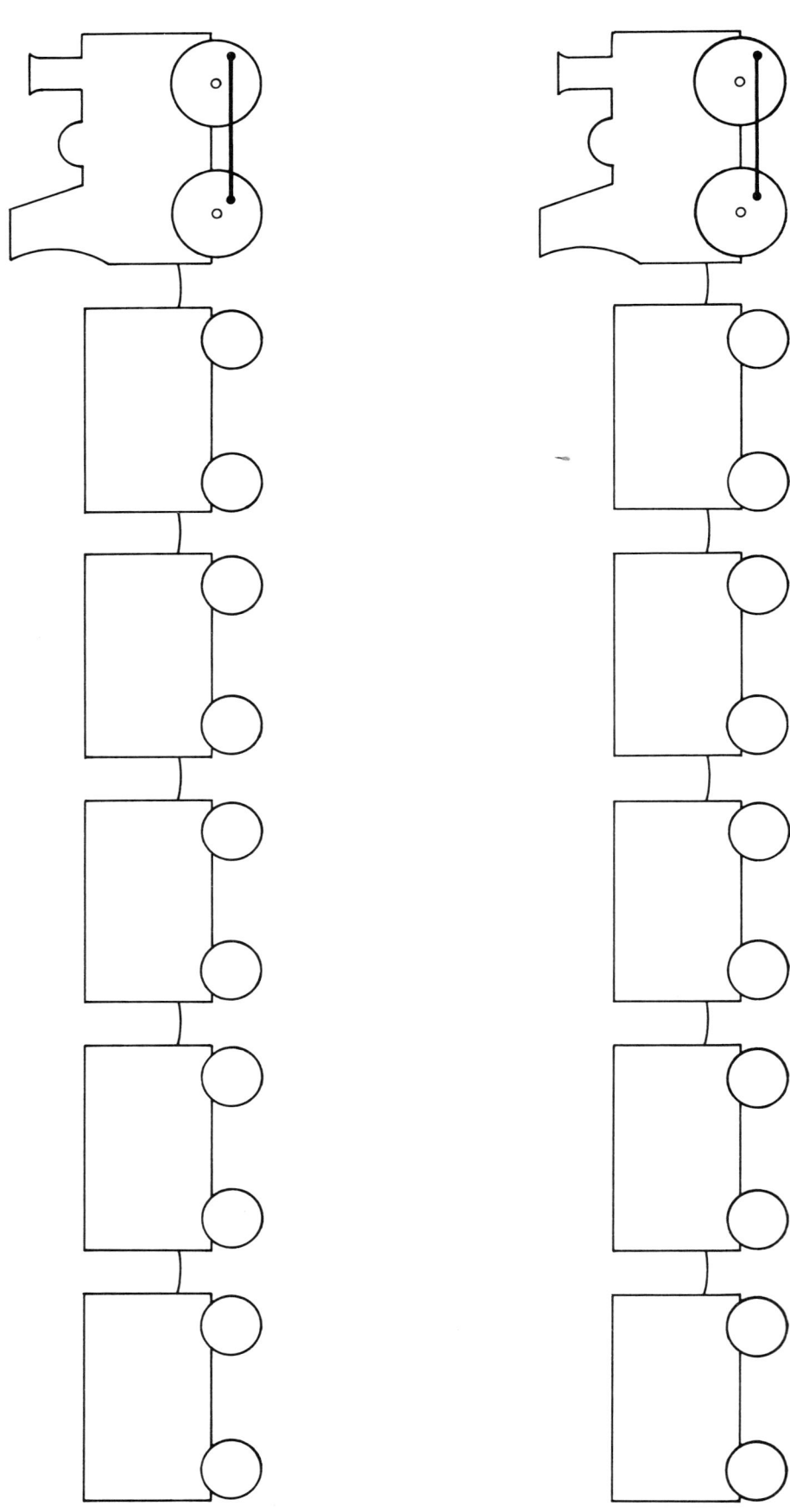

The 5 cat   The five cat

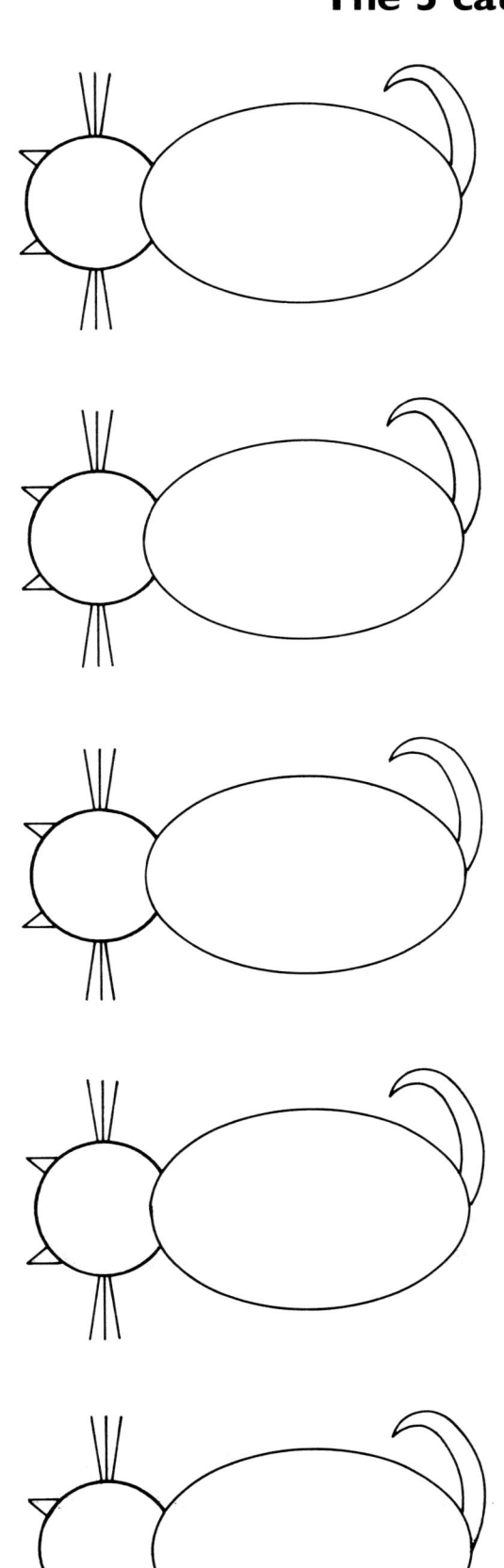
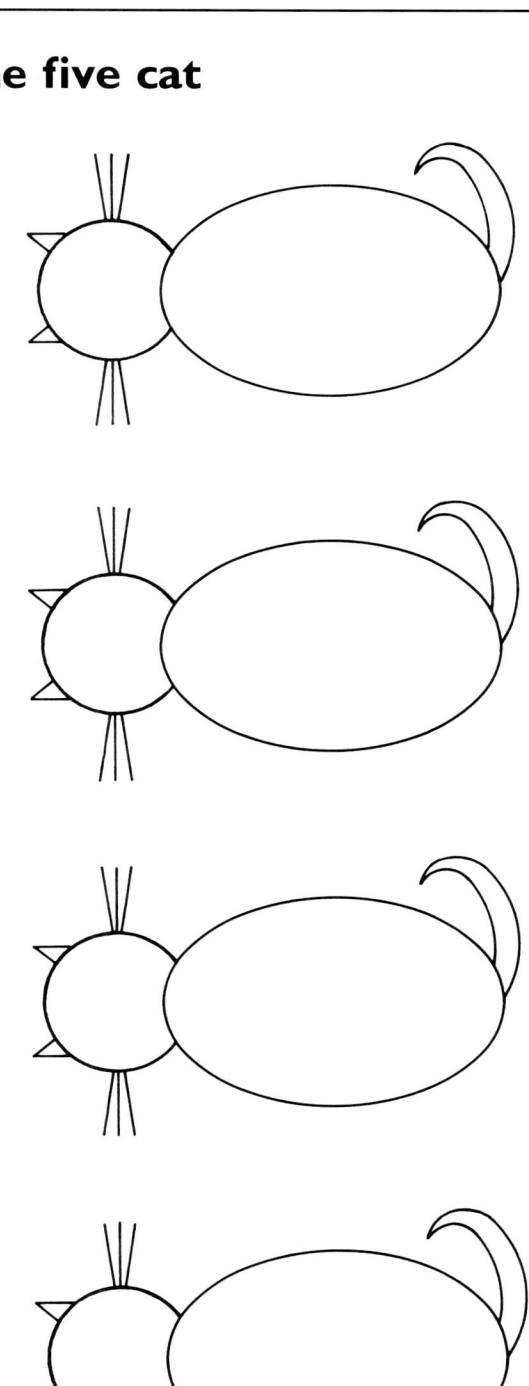
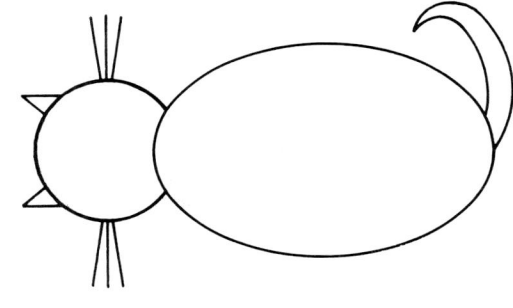
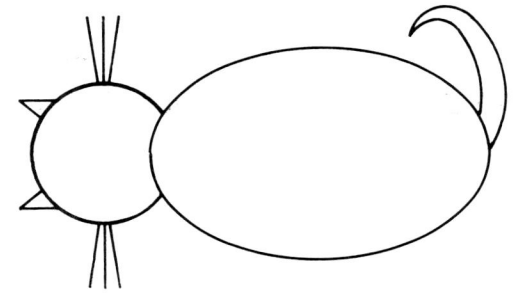

The 5 fish   The five fish

Making numbers (Limited entry)

I could use these keys.

I made ⬭ like this _____

I made ⬭ like this _____

I made ⬭ like this _____

I made ⬭ like this _____

I made ⬭ like this _____

I made ⬭ like this _____

I made ⬭ like this _____

I made ⬭ like this _____

Magic Arithmegons

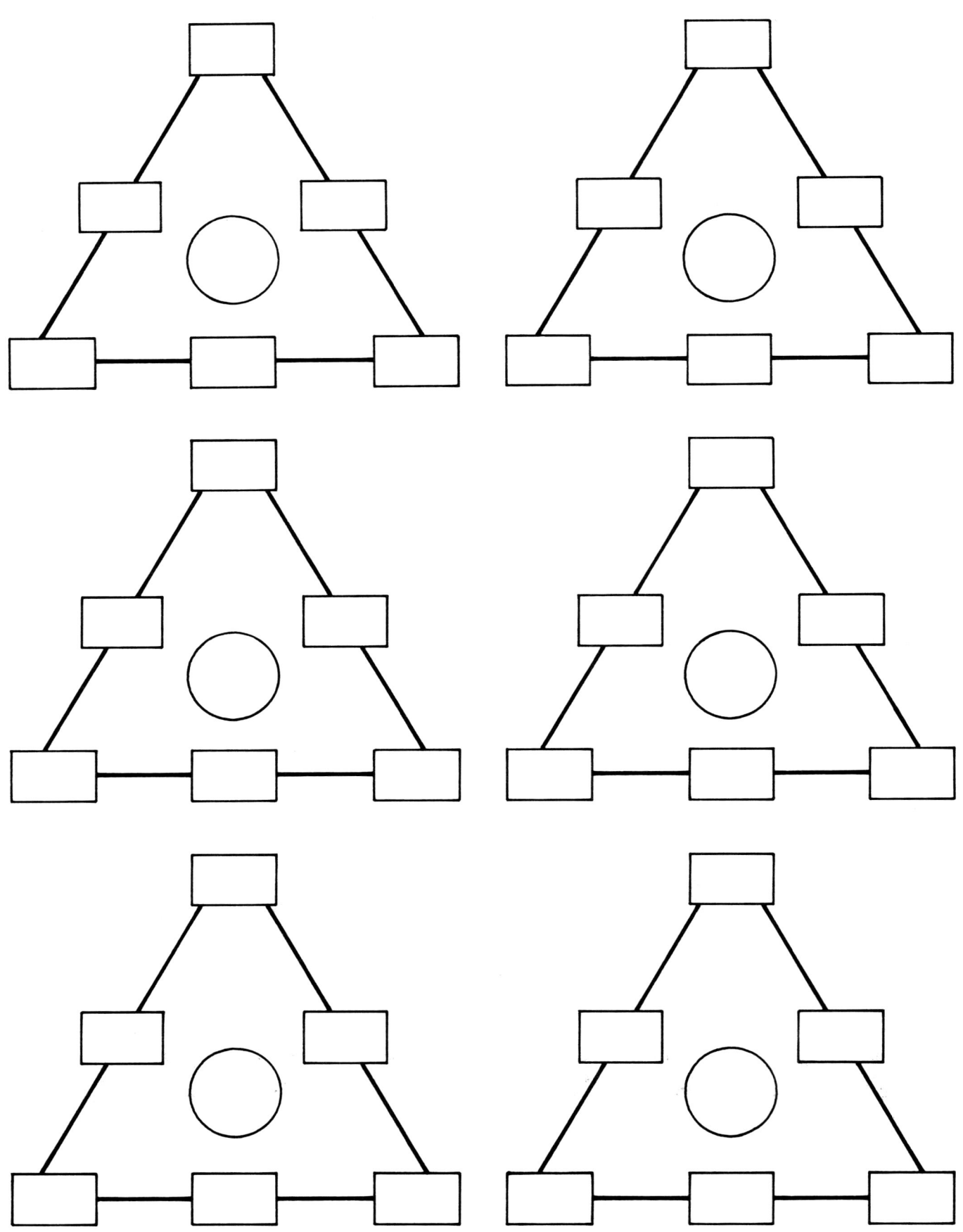

Polyominoes

Noah's Ark

Arithmegon game card

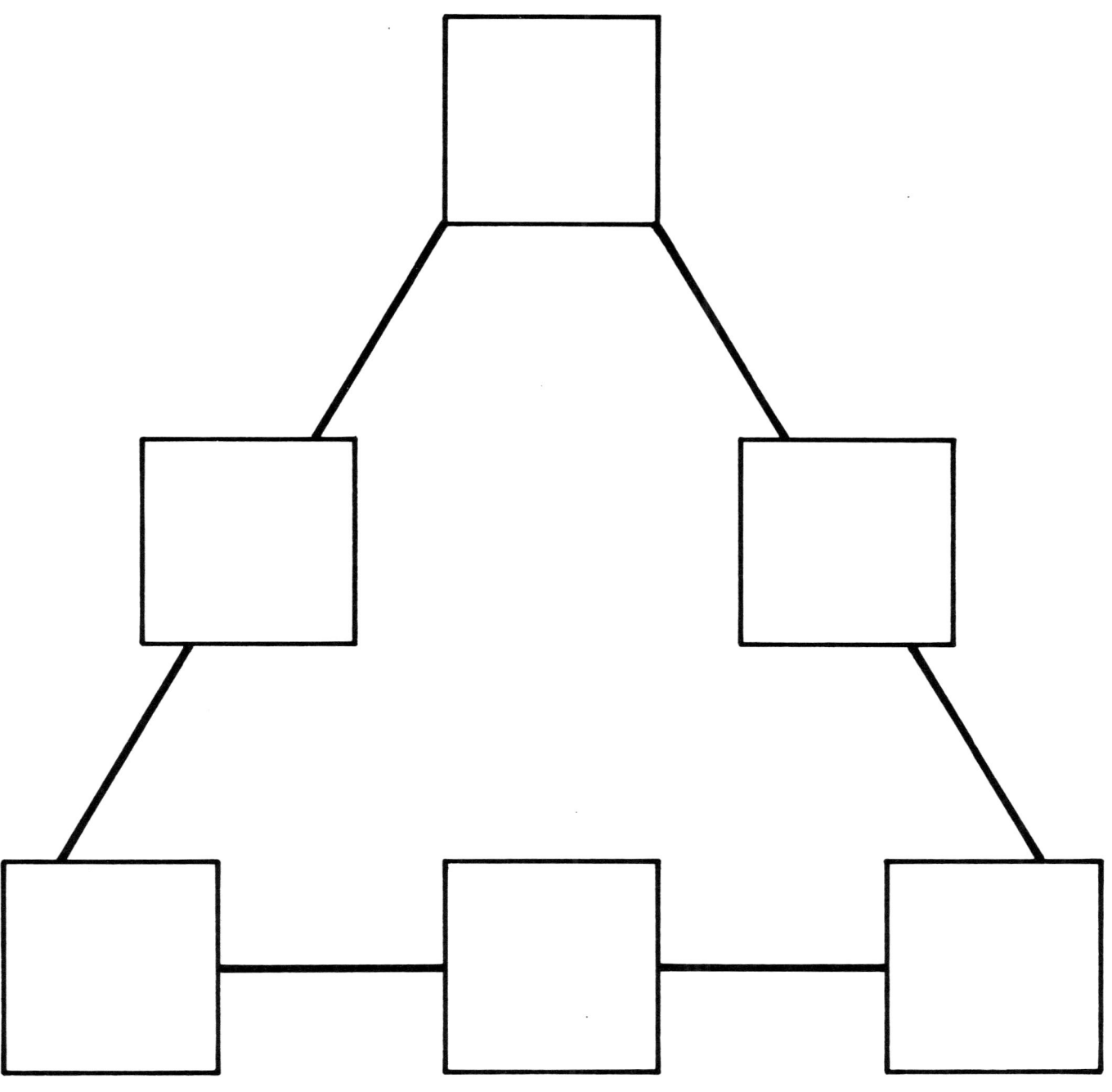

Digit cards

1	2	3	4	5	6
1	2	3	4	5	6
1	2	3	4	5	6
1	2	3	4	5	6
1	2	3	4	5	6
1	2	3	4	5	6
1	2	3	4	5	6
1	2	3	4	5	6